THE TIMELINE OF
DISCOVERY
AND
INVENTION

INTRODUCTION
by Isaac Asimov

Today's scientists think that the universe started 15,000 million years ago with a vast explosion. They call this the 'Big Bang'. When it happened, all the matter in the universe was flung as dust and gas from one point in space and is still travelling outwards. After many millions of years, clumps of dust and gas gathered into gigantic clouds and condensed to form vast solid lumps. Countless numbers of these lumps were big enough to be squeezed by their own gravity until they became suns. Smaller lumps formed around them to become planets.

Our solar system was formed like this 4,600 million years ago. Earth became a planet 100 million years later. Living things first appeared on its surface 2,625 million years ago. *Homo sapiens,* as we call human beings like ourselves, have lived here for only about 50,000 years. If you could squeeze the whole of Earth's lifetime into 24 hours, mankind would exist for only the last second.

Homo sapiens (it means 'wise man') were very different from any life form that had gone before. They were clever. They learned to use stone and wooden tools, which helped them to gather and prepare food, build shelters, cut firewood and provide skins for clothing. Tools were also used as weapons to defend their small wandering groups against wild animals and to conquer other tribes' hunting grounds.

Homo sapiens could do something else that other animals could not. They could think and were curious. While successful hunters and warriors proudly boasted of their bravery and victories around the cooking-fires, others asked questions about themselves, life and the world around them. Answers to such questions often helped make life easier for all mankind. Yet when the thinkers had invented writing, it was first used to boast of wars and conquests, the rise and fall of kings and queens, civilizations and empires — but not the names of its inventors.

This book tells of mankind's attempts to make life better for everyone. Inventors and thinkers were not always rewarded for their efforts. There were times when one had to be brave to question existing ideas. Many inventors were mocked, imprisoned, tortured or killed because of their opinions.

Many new ideas were seen as dangerous to the rulers or priests of their day, yet they were so useful that those who understood them gained almost magical powers over the rest of their fellows. The skill of reading and writing, for example, remained the secret of priests and rulers for over 8,000 years until the invention of printing brought it to the public. The idea of the formation of the universe described in the first paragraph of this Introduction was thought foolish when announced thirty years ago. It would have been

thought madness a century ago, Godless a century before, and anyone suggesting it in AD 1400 might well have been burned alive for devil worship or witchcraft.

Attempts to suppress knowledge have never succeeded; information spread all the faster. While great scientists knew that their ideas often came from something seen or heard before. Sir Isaac Newton said that his 1686 theory of gravity was based on 'the work of the giants who went before me'. James Watt admitted that his first steam engine was an improvement on Newcomen's 1712 'atmospheric engine'.

This timeline book plots the rapid growth of human knowledge over more than 50,000 years. At the beginning little changed but as we near the present day, more and more is known. Twice as much was learned between 1500 and 1800 as had been discovered previously. The next two hundred years has doubled it again. Among recent inventions are those that help us date and understand the discoveries of the past, thus enabling us to compile this Timeline. We are always learning, so some of the early dates may still vary in accuracy.

Mankind now possesses the knowledge to destroy or save our planet. We all hope that scientists will work for a safe future for the Earth and that we shall not see the end of 4,500 million years of world history.

PETER NORTH AND PHILIP WILKINSON

GALAHAD JR. BOOKS
NEW YORK

How to use this book

The Timeline of Discovery and Invention covers the history of invention from the earliest days of mankind to the present — over 50,000 years. The superbly illustrated timeline chart runs throughout the book to give a panoramic view of what was invented where, when and by whom. In between, indicated by the arrows, gatefold pages can be opened out to reveal yet more fascinating facts, figures and information.

The dating system is one used in many countries of the world today: the year 1 is the year that Jesus Christ was said to have been born. Dates before that are marked BC (meaning before Christ). Very often historians cannot be sure exactly when an event took place, and names and other details have been lost. Sometimes the letter *c* appears in front of a date — this is short for a Latin word *circa* meaning 'about' or 'approximate' and shows that the date is uncertain.

Some inventions are claimed by several people as their own ideas, while the discoverers of others remain anonymous. Often ideas started in one part of the world spread to other areas and an idea begun by one person may have been developed by others.

You can use the book in three different ways:

You can simply turn over the pages of the timeline chart to look at two pages of discovery and invention at a time and see what was happening where and when.

Or, as you go along, you can open up the left-hand pages and follow the story of discovery across three pages to see even more at once.

More information Meanwhile, if you open up the right-hand pages, as indicated by the arrows in the margins, you will find lots more information, facts, figures and stories about what was happening in the world at that time. Some exciting inventions are described in more detail and bring the past to life as you read.

All the ideas and discoveries in the timeline chart are divided into thirteen separate kinds by coloured bands which are explained in the key on the right. Use the timeline to compare progress in all these areas at one point in history, or follow a band along the chart to see the development of one kind of human inventiveness, such as in transport or medicine, and see how this has shaped the world we know today.

The original wall chart was compiled, designed and illustrated by
Peter North

Design of Timeline and additional pages
David Playne

Additional illustrations
Peter North
Christos Kondeatis
Patrick Wright

Text for additional Timeline pages
Philip Wilkinson

General Editors
Gill Davies
Del Tucker

ISBN 0 88394 973 3

First published in the U.S. by Galahad Jr. Books. Galahad Jr. Books is a division of Budget Book Service, Inc. 386 Park Avenue South, New York New York 10016

Copyright © 1993 Studio Editions

Printed and bound in Singapore

Ideas and Discoveries
Human exploration of the environment and the growth of civilization

Counting and Communications
The development of communication from counting and speech to computers and videos

Matter and Materials
The discovery and growing understanding of the materials we use, natural and manmade

Structures and Buildings
How buildings and machines have been made, from the mud-hut to the 100 storey skyscraper

Tools and Manufacturing
The devices mankind has used to make and do many things

Fuel and Power
From manpower, fire and water to rocket fuel

Machines and Engines
How humans have used machines to help perform tasks beyond human strength

Farming and Fishing
The development of people's attempts to feed themselves

Weapons and Defence
The devices mankind has used to protect himself and his community from attack

Transport and Travel
The development of fast, safe and comfortable transport, from wheeled carts to Concorde

Home Life
How everyday living has become more comfortable – from cooking-pots to microwave ovens

Health and Medicine
The growing understanding of the human body, and of cures for diseases and injuries

Culture and Entertainment
Humanity's interest in art, literature, music and games

World History
World events and the discoveries and inventions which affected them

The first inventions

Boats and rafts

A boat and a swimming float made of animal skins, used about 3,000 years ago

No one knows when the first watercraft were made. They probably began when people realized they could use naturally buoyant objects to help them swim. It was then only a small step forward to begin using these to make a raft on which to travel. Early rafts were made by lashing together logs or bundles of reeds. In some places inflated animal skins were used as swimming floats and these were also attached to rafts to make them more buoyant. In the 7th century BC the Assyrians depicted rafts with such floats but marine historians think that their use goes back much further.

The dugout canoe — a boat made from a log that has been hollowed out using fire and axes — also appeared very early. Examples from as early as 6300 BC have been found, and British archaeologists have unearthed a paddle dating from 7500 BC.

By the 4th millennium BC craft had become highly sophisticated in some parts of the world. In Egypt, for example, well-made reed rafts were propelled and steered using oars; the Egyptians also developed the use of sails. In northern Europe, frame-built boats appeared, with a covering of animal skin stretched across a lightweight wooden frame. Called coracles in Wales and Ireland, and quffas in western Asia, these boats are still used today.

The wheel

Before the wheel, people had to push heavy loads along on rollers, use sledges, or drag them along using a framework. But in the 4th millennium BC in Mesopotamia, the wheel was invented. Our first evidence for this is a pictogram from the city of Erech (in modern Iraq) showing a four-wheeled cart which looks like an adapted sledge. This image dates from about 3500 BC. The earliest surviving wheeled vehicles come from Ur, south-east of Erech. These are about 1,000 years later in date.

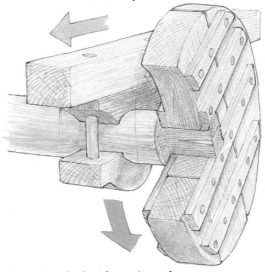

An early wheel with turning axle

These early wheels were made of wood. They usually consisted of three planks joined by cross-pieces. The middle of the central plank was left thicker and carved to make a hub. The wheel was probably one of those inventions that spread around the world from a single place. Wheels with similar structures from about 2000 BC have been found as far afield as India, Crete and Russia.

Later developments of the wheel made it lighter; first some of the wood was removed by cutting holes in the planks; then the wooden wheels were made with thick spokes. Metal was also used — often to reinforce the rim of the wheel.

Two designs of axles were used with early wheels. In one type the axle was fixed rigidly to the body of the cart and the wheel turned on the axle. In the other the wheel and axle were fixed rigidly together and both turned.

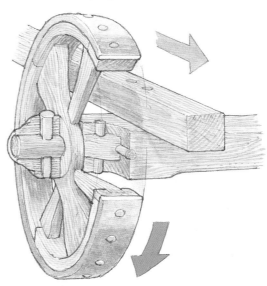

A wheel which turns on a fixed axle

An early ceremonial cart which would have been pushed by people unseen by the dignitaries riding inside

Timekeeping

In early societies, people knew all they needed to know about the time from the position of the Sun in the sky. If it was light, they could work in the fields; if it was dark, it was time to sleep. But the ancient Egyptians learned to tell the time more accurately from the Sun. They developed the shadow clock. This was a T-shaped stick with the cross-bar slightly raised. The time was indicated by the position of the shadow of the cross-bar on numbers along the stem. In other words, the shadow clock was a form of sundial.

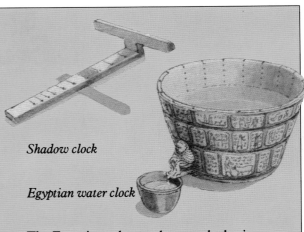

Shadow clock

Egyptian water clock

The Egyptians also used water clocks, in which the flow of water through a tiny hole indicated the time. This was rather like the hourglass of later periods. Both of these devices were in use by about 1000 BC.

Pyramids

The ancient Egyptians were the first people to build on a large scale in stone. Their temples, and the pyramids beneath in which some of their rulers are buried, are so large that people often wonder how they managed to move the

massive stones with the primitive technology available to them between about 2686 and 1777 BC, when the pyramids were built.

Tutankhamen

Born about 1371 BC and died when he was only 19 years old, having been pharaoh of Egypt for nine years. His fame spread after his tomb was discovered in 1922. The survival of such burial riches was unique; royal tombs in Egypt were plundered almost as soon as they were built! His was hidden by rubble during the building of Rameses VI's tomb.

Did you know that . . .

Etruscan dentists were making false teeth in 700 BC.

The Egyptians were one of the earliest people to invent letter forms. From highly pictorial hieroglyphics they developed a more simplified script so that their scribe could write more quickly.

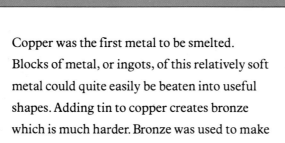

How did the pyramid builders do it?

They used river transport to move the stone as close to the building site as they could.

Sledges were probably used to move the materials from the boats to the site itself.

As the pyramid walls grew higher, it is thought that the builders made a system of spiral earth ramps and dragged the stones up these. The ramps extended in a gradual slope all the way around the pyramid, and would have to be added to as the structure grew.

All the earth would have to be removed at the end of the construction — a task almost as hard as bringing the stone to the site in the first place!

Metalworking

The first metalworkers probably beat gold nuggets into shape to make small objects. But gold is a rare metal and metalworking on a large scale could begin only when people discovered how to smelt — to extract metal from rock by heating it. This discovery was made independently in different places and at different times. In some places in western Asia and southeast Europe smelting began as early as 6000 BC. By 2000 BC smelting was being practised elsewhere in Europe and Asia, as well as in Africa.

Copper was the first metal to be smelted. Blocks of metal, or ingots, of this relatively soft metal could quite easily be beaten into useful shapes. Adding tin to copper creates bronze which is much harder. Bronze was used to make more durable tools and weapons.

The molten metal produced by smelting was at first left to cool and solidify, after which it could be hammered into shape. But molten metal can also be cast — poured into a mould to produce a ready-made object of the required shape. Bronze happens to be a good material for casting, so cast-bronze tools and

weapons began to appear. This process was ideal for creating the sort of solid objects (such as axeheads) which had previously been made in stone.

Between 2000 and 1500 BC in western Asia another great leap forward in metalworking occurred: the use of iron. Iron is a more common metal than the copper and tin needed to make bronze. Iron blades also take a sharp edge very well. So ironworking spread quickly after 1500 BC and iron became the usual material from which to make all but the most luxurious tools and weapons.

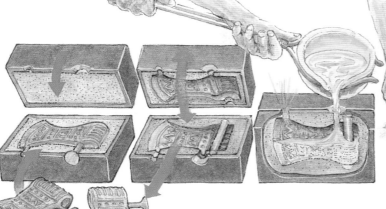

The development of metalwork		
Earliest times		Gold is beaten
6000 BC	Western Asia	Smelting begins
	South-East Europe	
2000 BC	Europe	Smelting of copper
	Asia	Tin is added to copper
	Africa	to make bronze
2000-500 BC	Western Asia	Ironworking develops

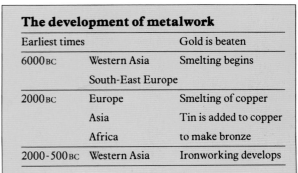

- By 1860, one of the last unknown continents, **Africa**, had been crossed by explorers.
  Caillié 1828
  Speke/Burton 1863
  Livingstone 1873
  Nachtigal 1874
  Stanley 1877

- 1863 Galton's book *Meteorographica* established the theory of **anticyclones.**

- 1876 Dewey's decimal **library classification** system coded books by subject.

- 1884 A line through the Observatory at Greenwich became the zero line of longitude, with local time known as **GMT.**

- 1891 Hale's **spectroheliograph** made it possible to study the sun's spectrum and the nature of stars.

- 1895 Röntgen discovered **X-rays**, electromagnetic waves which travel through flesh but not bone.

- 1873 Clerk Maxwell stated that heat, light and electricity are all **electro magnetic waves.**

- 1876 Bell patented the **telephone** (right). Sound made a diaphragm vibrate, and was transmitted as electrical signals along a wire.

- In the 1880s Hollerith developed an information processing system, using **hole-punched cards**, for the US Bureau of Census.
  (left) Hollerith punched card

- 1887-88 Hertz detected the existence of **radio waves.**

- 1888 Eastman made photographic **roll film.**

- 1892 An automatic **telephone exchange** allowing direct dialling was built in the US, using Strowger's selector.

- 1869 First **colour photograph** displayed.

- 1877 Edison invented the **phonograph**, to record and play back sound, using a needle on a tin foil cylinder.

- 1894 The first 'moving' pictures were shown on Edison's **kinetoscope**, a kind of peep-show.

- 1894 The Lumière brother's **cine-camera** and projector made and showed films.

- 1888 Eastman's Kodak **Brownie** camera made photography cheap, simple and popular.

Machines were built using **lithography** to print paper from flat stone blocks.

- 1866 Brunel's iron ship *Great Eastern* laid an underwater **transatlantic telegraph cable** (above).

- 1867 Sholes and Gidden in the US built the first practical **typewriter**, made from **1874** by the gunmakers, Remington.

- 1886 Doehring strengthened cement with steel wires to make **pre-stressed concrete.**
  The **Forth Rail Bridge** was built in Scotland in the 1880s, using 58,000 tonnes of steel.

- 1884 **Acrylic** was patented, but its importance for making plastics and resins was not yet recognized.

- 1884 Chardonnet used plant cellulose to make the artificial fibre, **rayon**, which provided silky thread.

- 1896 Becquerel found **radioactivity** in the metal uranium. The radioactive elements **radium** and **polonium** were discovered by the Curies in Paris.
  Many objects could be made from the new plastics.

- 1860 Parkes produced the first **plastic** - Parkesine - by dissolving cellulose in nitric acid.

- 1869 Russian chemist Mendeleyev published his **Periodic Table** of elements, refining the work of Dalton.

- 1869 Hyatt made a strong inflammable plastic, called **celluloid.**

- The 1882 Montauk Building, the first **skyscraper**, had only 10 storeys. Another Chicago building of 1884-85 had a lighter **steel riveted frame.**

- 1884 **Revolving doors** in skyscrapers did not stick shut in draughts caused by **elevators.**

- 1889 The erection of the 320 m **Eiffel Tower** showed the building heights possible with wrought iron frames.

A new plastic was developed from a by-product of milk–**casein.**

- 1863 Nobel first made **explosives** of nitroglycerine, and in 1867 invented **dynamite.** Later, gelignite and the more stable **TNT** were developed.

- 1869 De Lesseps' **Suez Canal**, a 170 km waterway, was opened.
  Mediterranean
  Port Said
  Suez Canal

- 1868 Mayo patented uses for his strong sheets of hot-glued veneers: **plywood.**

- 1889 A dam built across the Willamette River produced hydro-electric power in Oregon.

- 1895 Fein made the first hand-held **electric drill** in Germany.
  Engineering workshops turned from steam power to electricity to drive increased numbers of **automatic machine tools**, which could follow a programme to make different objects without being adjusted by hand.

- 1867 Monnier embedded iron bars in **reinforced concrete** to make it a stronger, more versatile building material.

- 1878 Victoria Embankment, London, was Britain's first street to be lit by **electric arc lights.**

- 1892 Dewar's two-walled **vacuum flask** kept liquids cold or hot (right).

- 1862 Brown's universal milling machine made possible the quick and precise mass production of tools.

- 1886 Thomson took out a patent for an electric arc **welder** in the US.

- 1880 Nyberth's **blow torch**, burned air and gas to create intense heat (right).

- 1884 Beart's steam-powered **rotary drill** meant that oil wells could be drilled faster and deeper.

- 1891 **Oil cracking** was invented; an oil-refining process which enabled fuel and other products to be distilled from crude oil.

- 1865 Von Syckel's **oil pipeline** ran 8 km from Pennsylvania oil field to railway loading point.

- 1873 Developing Faraday's earlier work on electricity, the Gramme industrial **dynamo** generated power in the Gramme factory, Paris.

- 1880 Pelton's **turbine** was driven by a high-speed water jet hitting scoops to turn a wheel.

- 1879 Planté's 20-year old idea for a **rechargeable** storage **battery** finally became practical with the work of Faure.

- The *Gluckauf*, launched in 1886, was fitted with tanks to hold oil.
  Gluckauf oil tanker

- 1891 An **electric car** built by Morris and Salom ran non-stop for 13 hours.

- 1867-69 Bergès used water to generate **hydro-electric power**, which he called 'white coal'.

- 1878 Gramme in France and Siemens in Germany manufactured electrical **alternators.**

- 1885 Daimler designed a petrol engine which he fitted to a small motorcycle which ran at 8 kmh.

- 1890 Stuart's **compression ignition engine** detonated fuel by air heated through compression in the cylinder.

Turbinia

- Slater's 1864 **drive chain** became a very important feature of industry.

- 1878 In Otto's **internal combustion engine**, coal, gas and air exploded in a cylinder to push a piston and turn a drive wheel.

- 1892 The **diesel engine** used less refined fuel - now known as diesel.

- 1897 Parsons converted his steam turbine to drive a ship at 34.5 knots, faster than any other at the time (above).

- 1873 Glidden's **barbed wire** produced cheap, effective fencing.
  Pea plants proved Mendel's theories.

- 1884 Parson's high-pressure steam turbine produced a great deal of power. Steam passing through a series of blades forced a shaft to turn at very high speeds.

- 1878 Clerk designed a **two-stroke engine**, later simplified.

- 1880 **Windmills** produced electricity in the US.

- 1872 Foyn's **harpoon gun** mounted on ships was used in the whaling industry.

- 1885 Mendel's **theory of inheritance** showed that offspring inherit a set of 'instructions', or **genes**, from their parents.

- 1868 Higham's **sheep shears** could mechanically fleece animals very quickly.

- 1878 De Laval's **cream separator** used a turbine to spin cream from milk.

- 1878 Colvin's **milking machine** sucked milk from the cow's udder by vacuum.

The horse-drawn **potato-digger** was widely used.

- 1892 Froelich's petrol-driven **tractor**, though not a success, marked a great step forward in farming, and was improved by Albone ten years later.

- 1892 Ivanovsky discovered the first **viruses** while studying diseases found in tobacco plants.

- 1860 The Winchester **repeating rifle** was fed by a lever from a magazine (above).
  'Volcanic action' lever

- 1866 Whitehead's underwater missile - the **torpedo** (below).

- 1880 Garratt designed a **steam-powered submarine** with a retractable chimney. In 1888 *Gymnote*, an experimental naval submarine, was launched.

- 1884 Maxim made the first machine **gun**, which used a bullet's recoil to feed it the next round.

- 1884 **Cordite**, a smokeless explosive made of nitroglycerine and guncotton, was used to fire shells from guns.

- 1877 (right) Ship **mine** with Hertz triggers.

- 1870 Riders of Starley's 'Penny Farthing' bicycle sat over the large front wheel to drive the fixed pedals.

- 1885 Starley's Rover **safety bicycle** had equal sized rubber wheels and a chain drive.

- 1888 Dunlop invented **air-filled rubber tyres**, making cycling far more comfortable.

- 1890 The first **electric underground trains** ran under London.

- 1886 Daimler produced the first petrol-driven four-wheel **car**. He later joined forces with fellow engineer Benz.

- 1860 Wooden warships such as *HMS Warrior* were sheathed in thick **iron cladding.**

- 1876 **Plimsoll lines** (left) on ship's hulls to show safe loading levels became law.
  Plimsoll line

- (above) 1879 Siemen designed the first **electric tram.**

- 1863 London's first **underground railway** had steam locomotives and windowless carriages.

- 1868 A **traffic light** was in use in London, showing only red or green.

- 1891 Lilienthal experimented with an unpowered flying machine made of wood and cloth - the first **hang-glider.** He controlled it using his body weight.

- 1860 Walton invented a hard floor covering known as **linoleum.**

- 1860 Newnham invented the **press-stud fastener.**

- 1868 More homes installed gas when Maughan designed a **water heater** with a gas burner.

- 1879 Edison and Swan both designed a **light bulb** which burned a carbon filament in a vacuum. They joined forces to make and sell the device.

- 1887 Pemberton worked out the formula for the drink **Coca-Cola**, as a medical tonic.

- 1889 Mrs Cockran made a **dishwasher**, which sprayed water on dishes stacked in a tub.

- 1893 The first breakfast cereal was Perky's Shredded Wheat.

- 1876 Bissell invented a hand operated **carpet sweeper**, with a rotating brush.

- 1874 Fox made the steel rib **umbrella.**

- 1886 Corrosion-free **aluminium saucepans** were produced by Hall's electrolyte process.

- 1891 Judson invented the **zip fastener.**

- 1895 Röntgen took an X-ray of his wife's hand. X-rays were soon used for diagnosis (below).

- 1869 Chemically **self-raising flour** went on sale.

- 1867 Lister performed an **antiseptic** operation, using a carbolic acid spray on wounds to kill germs.

- 1879 Linde's Alaska **refrigerator** was a wooden box cooled by ice.

- 1885 Pasteur developed the first effective **vaccine** against rabies.

- 1885 The **epidural anaesthetic** was devised to deaden the pelvic organs.

- 1895 Freud published his book on **psychoanalysis** - a new approach to mental illness, based on identifying repressed feelings.

- 1863 Harrington's clockwork **dental drill** made mending teeth easier, but no less painful.

- 1859 Billiards championships were held in Detroit. The game spread, and **snooker and pool** were developed.

- 1877 Manson showed mosquitoes spread disease.

- 1884 A local anaesthetic was developed, using cocaine.

- 1887 Frick made glass **contact lenses.**

- 1893 A German chemist marketed **aspirin**, using it to treat rheumatism.

- 1860 Pasteur showed that **bacteria** could be destroyed by heat without affecting the taste of food, by the process **pasteurisation.**

- 1876 An **ice rink**, called the Glacerium, opened in London.

- 1878 **Electric lighting** began to be used inside and outside theatres.

- 1887 Berliner designed a hand-powered **gramophone.** Sounds were stored on flat zinc-coated discs or cylinders.

- 1889 **Table tennis** was invented by Gibb, and sold as 'Ping Pong'.

- 1897 Votey created the **pianola**, a piano which played by itself, using music written on perforated paper.

- In the 1860s Fenby's piano firm sold a device which could write music being played on a piano.

- 1882 A school of 'judo' (gentle way) opened in Tokyo and the sport was spread by emigrants.

- 1897 **Plasticene**, a non-setting modelling clay, was invented by Harbutt.

The Netherlands
Great Britain *Belgium*
France *Germany*
Russia
Austro-Hungary
Spain *Italy* *Romania*
Portugal *The Balkans*
Switzerland *Greece*
Ottoman Turks

- 1860-70 With the arrival of steam, there was a boom in railway building. Railways became the major means of transporting goods and people, as their nations became industrialised.

- 1867 Marx's book *Das Kapital* suggested that wealth was created by workers, not owners, and became the basis of communism.

European countries raced to set up colonies around the world, particularly in Africa and the Far East, to increase trade and obtain cheap labour and raw materials.

- In 1882 European powers made alliances which divided them into two camps: Germany, Austro-Hungary and Italy versus Britain, France and Russia.

The **Ottoman Empire**, ruled by Turkey, declined, and disputes over the Balkan states worsened.

- 1889 The introduction of a constitution in Japan marked the end of its feudal way of life, as western trade and ideas gained acceptance.

By 1870 there were large national railway networks in many countries (see above).

1900 · 1905 · 1910 · 1915 · 1920 · 1925

• 1900 Planck's **quantum theory** of energy stated that energy in atoms acts in tiny fixed units, called 'quanta'.

• 1901 Heaviside predicted the existence of a layer of the atmosphere which reflects radio signals. This **Heaviside layer** was located in 1925.

• 1905 In Einsteins' **special theory of relativity**, light speed is constant: time passes at different rates for objects in constant relative motion. Atomic power was predicted in the formula $E = mc^2$.

Albert Einstein

• 1915 Einstein published his **general theory of relativity**, which examined the relationship between time and space.

• 1911 Onnes discovered **superconductivity**: the drop in electrical resistance of certain metals at very low temperatures.

• 1912 Leavitt's **Cepheid variables** allowed for Hubble's 1923 theory of an expanding universe.

• 1919 Rutherford's investigation into the structure of atoms led to his 1911 discovery of the **atomic nucleus** and then to the first experiment in **atomic fission**, or splitting the atom.

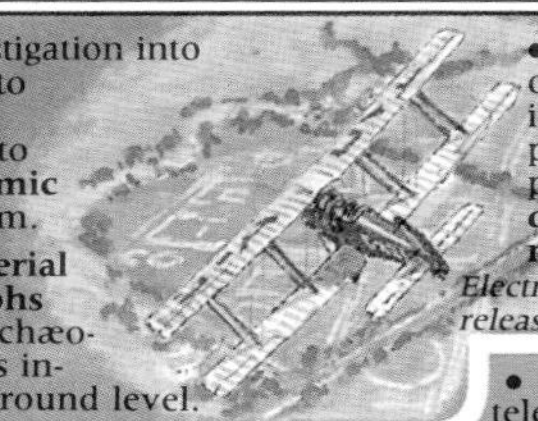

• 1924 **Aerial photographs** showed archæological sites invisible at ground level.

• 1927 De Broglies' theor of 1924 that subatomic par icles behave like waves wa proved by experiments in **quantum mechanics.**

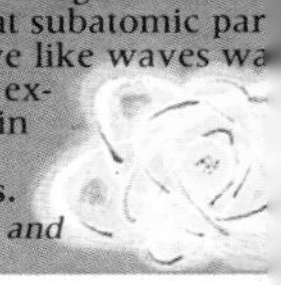
Electrons 'jump' and release energy

• 1901 Marconi proved that **radio waves** followed the curve of the earth, and demonstrated long-range transmissions by sending the Morse code signal for 'S' from Cornwall to Newfoundland.

Guglielmo Marconi

• 1906 Fessenden invented AM radio and made the first spoken **radio broadcast**.

• 1911 Monroe invented a **comptometer calculator** which could multiply and divide by the turn of a handle. Mass produced office comptometers were made in France from 1920.

• 1914 Barnack exhibited a revolutionary small, hand-held camera, which the Leitz Co. improved to launch as the **Leica** (below) in **1925**.

Nellie Melba recording

• 1925 Maxfield perfected an electrical system of **recording** using a microphone.

• 1920 East Pittsburgh's KDKA **radio station** began broadcasting.

• 1925 Logie Baird's mecha television system and Zworyk electronic iconoscope de heralded the sta televis

• 1930 Baird's expe mental TV transmiss began but were overtaken by the US **electronic system.**

• 1903 The work of the Curies and Becquerel on **radioactivity** won them the Nobel Prize.

• 1905 Wood patented non-shatter **safety glass** and fitted it to his car.

• 1908 The thin plastic film Cellophane was made, and by **1912** was sold as a food covering.

• 1909 Baekeland, from Belgium invented **Bakelite**, the first plastic made from synthetic chemicals.

• 1913 The heat-proof plastic laminate **formica** was manufactured in the US.

• 1913 Brearley produced **stainless steel** by adding chromium and nickel to prevent rusting.

• 1913 The 60-storey Woolworth building appeared on the New York skyline, designed in gothic style by Gilbert.

1912 Baekeland invented a strong **synthetic wood glue**.

• 1915 **Pyrex** heat-resistant glass, which could cope with very high temperatures, found many uses in industry and in the home.

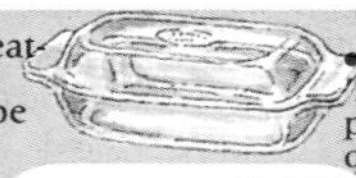

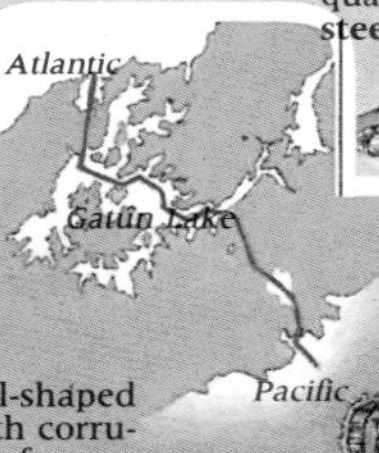

• 1914 The 80 km **Panama Canal** linked the Atlantic and Pacific Oceans.

• 1923 The continuous **'hot strip' mill** (below) produced larger quantities of **steel**.

• Many domestic and industrial items were made from colourful **urea formaldehyde plastics.**

• 1924 **Cellulose paints** were first used in the car industry.

• Polyvinyl chl **(PVC)** was first duced in Mosco **1912**, and in th US in **1928**.

• 1929 **Foam ru** was developed b Dunlop and used padding material

• The first **motorways** were the German Avus **autobahn** 1921, and the Italian Milan-Varese **Autostrada**, of 1926.

• 1928 A **clove intersectio** New Jersey n motorway junc

• 1902 Carrier's **air conditioner** cooled buildings by blowing air across cold water.

American architects built ever taller buildings with **curtain walls** fitted to light, strong frames.

• 1910 Claude's **neon lights** were soon used for signs in Paris.

• Tunnel-shaped Nissen huts with corrugated iron roofs were quick to build (left).

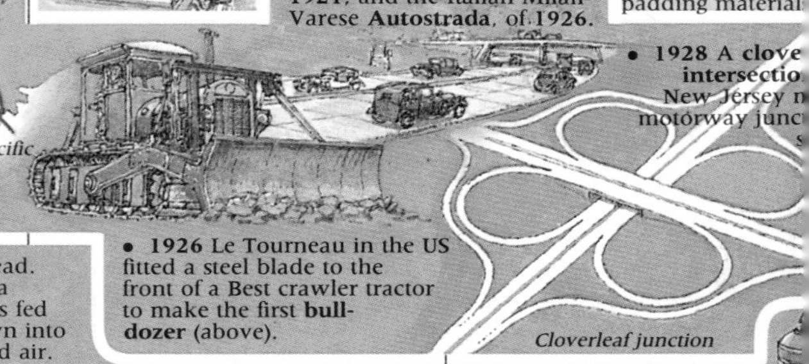

• 1926 Le Tourneau in the US fitted a steel blade to the front of a Best crawler tractor to make the first **bulldozer** (above).

Cloverleaf junction

• 1906 De Forest invented the **triode valve**, used in amplifiers until the transistor replaced it.

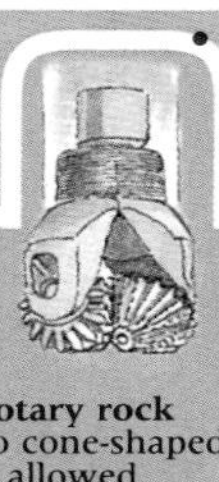

Valves were developed for many uses. They controlled electronic signals, helping to create, strengthen, combine or separate them.

• 1908 Ford founded his Motor Company and pioneered mass-production. By 1927, 15 million of his Model T cars had been made.

Mass production spread. In light bulb factories a ribbon of hot glass was fed along rollers and blown into shape with compressed air.

• 1904 Korn used Elster's **photoelectric cell** to scan photographs and send them by telegraph wire.

• 1909 The **rotary rock drill**, with two cone-shaped cutting heads, allowed deep drilling through the hardest rock (above).

• 1908 Edison invented a new kind of **dry-cell battery**, (below) using Leclanché's 1866 idea to produce a disposable energy storage device.

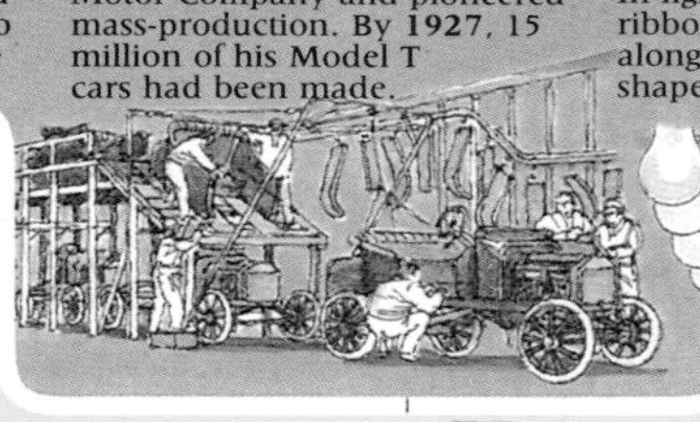

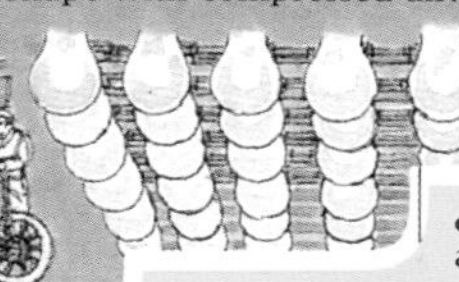

• 1921 Hall's **magnetron** generated short wavelength, high frequency waves, used in radar, and later, in microwaves.

• 1926 Rotheim's first **aerosol can** used pressurized air to spray out its contents.

• 1900 The first **offshore oil well** was drilled from a rig off Santa Barbara, on the coast of California, US.

• 1901 **Motor oil** marketed in UK.

• 1903 Tsiolkhovsky suggested using **liquid fuels** for rocket propulsion.

• 1905 **Gas turbines** produced massive power. The explosion of petrol burnt in compressed air turned the rotors.

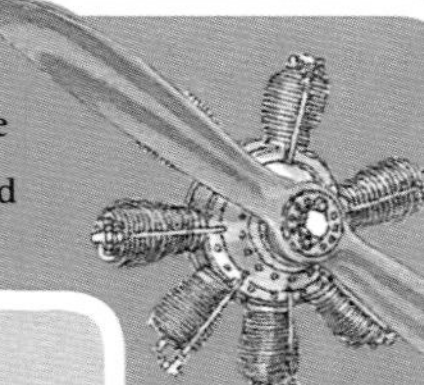

• 1912 Garfield invented a **hydraulic hoist** for tip trucks which was soon used world-wide.

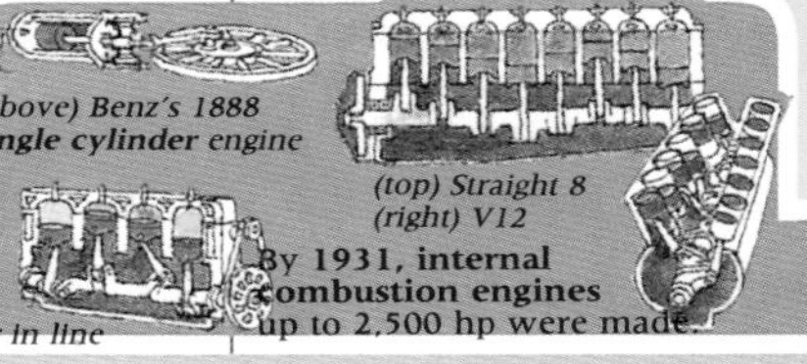

(above) Benz's 1888 **single cylinder** engine

(top) Straight 8 (right) V12

4-cylinder in line

By 1931, **internal combustion engines** up to 2,500 hp were made.

• 1920s Tetra-ethyl **lead** was added to petrol, to stop engines 'knocking'.

• 1924 Kattan invented a propeller-like **water-turbine** for hydro electric power stations.

• 1926 Goddard used petrol and liquid oxygen in his **liquid fuel rocket** (right).

• 1930 Houdry increased petrol yield from crude oil with a **catalytic cracker.**

• 1926 Goddard's first rocket reached a height of 56 m and a speed of 97 kmh.

• 1901 Lanchester invented the pre-selector **gearbox**, with four forward gears and reverse to ease vehicle control.

• 1912 Diesel electric generators were used to provide power for transport, houses and factories.

• 1907 Sequin made a 34hp Gnome **rotary aircraft engine** which spun to turn a propeller and cool the light engine.

• 1904 Holt's steam-powered **caterpillar tractor** was steered by driving the two tracks through separate clutches.

• 1917 Ford mass-produced the Fordson tractor, providing cheap, convenient power to farmers. Ten years later, 70,000 Fordsons a year were being built.

• 1921 The technique of **crop-spraying** was introduced when army pilots dusted trees in Ohio with insecticide.

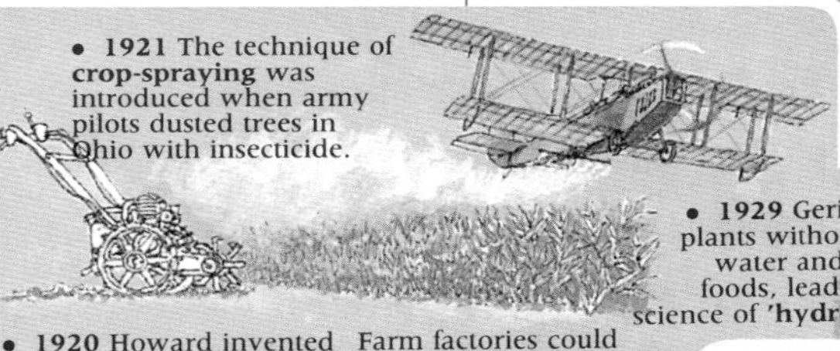

• 1913 **Nitrogen fertilizer** was made in Germany.

• 1929 Gericke plants without so water and esse foods, leading t science of **'hydropo**

• 1920 Howard invented a steam rotary hoe, with L-shaped blades, the first **Rotavator**.

Farm factories could freeze fresh food and transport it in refrigerated trains and ships.

• 1900 Zeppelin flew his new **airship**, a giant dangerously-flammable hydrogen filled balloon, driven by 4 engines.

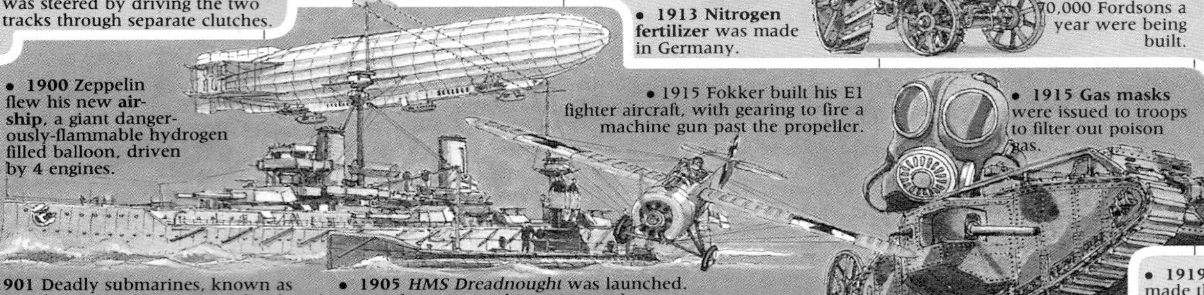

• 1915 Fokker built his E1 fighter aircraft, with gearing to fire a machine gun past the propeller.

• 1915 **Gas masks** were issued to troops to filter out poison gas.

• 1922 The Japanese navy built the *Hosho*, and the British *HMS Hermes* (right), the world's first purpose-built **aircraft carriers.**

• 1901 Deadly submarines, known as *unterseeboots* or **U-boats**, were developed for the German navy.

• 1905 *HMS Dreadnought* was launched. Driven by steam turbines, it was the first modern steel **battleship**.

• The British **tank**, a tracked, bullet-proof vehicle designed to cross ditches and climb banks, was used in battle in France in **1916**.

• 1919 Alcock and Brown made the first non-stop flight across the Atlantic while the Ross brothers flew from Britain to Australia.

• 1920 The Allies perfected ASDIC - an echo-sounder - to locate underwater objects and U-boats (now called **sonar**).

• 1923 De la Cierva flew h **autogyro**, a kind of helico with an unpowered rotor instead of an aeroplane's wings.

Wright's first flight covered 260m.

• 1912 The first **Diesel locomotives** were very slow but were quickly developed

• 1915 Junkers made an **all-metal aircraft** with unsupported wings, very advanced for its time.

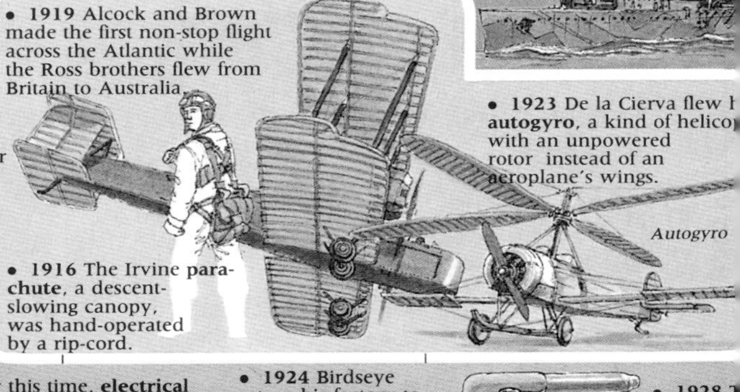
Autogyro

• 1916 The Irvine **parachute**, a descent-slowing canopy, was hand-operated by a rip-cord.

• 1903 Wright built an aeroplane and engine to make the first **controlled powered flight.**

• 1907 The first **helicopter**, Cornu's rotating wing aircraft, rose 60 cm above the ground.

• 1907 Spengler sold his patent for a **vacuum cleaner** to WH Hoover (below).

• 1901 The **safety razor** was patented by Gillette and Nickerson.

• 1907 **Detergent** was sold in Germany.

• 1913 Crosby made the first **brassiere** using ribbons to sew two silk handkerchiefs together.

• 1904 Automatic **tea-making machines** were advertized with the slogan 'A clock that makes tea!'

• 1912 A chain of **self-service** grocery stores opened in California.

By this time, **electrical appliances** available for the home included stoves, ovens, heaters, irons kettles and refrigerators.

• 1924 Birdseye set up his factory to freeze, package and sell **frozen food** to be thawed and cooked at home

• 1928 T **cellulose adhes tape**, Sellota was marke

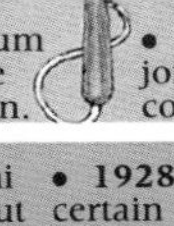

• 1925 An aluminium **hairdryer** was made with a heater and fan.

• 1927 Salad cream joined Heinz's list of convenience foods.

• 1906 Fisher designed an **electric washing machine**.

• 1910 **Gas fires** with fire-clay radiants were made.

• 1909 General Electric's **electric toaster** used red hot wires to toast bread.

(above) 1918 An electric **food mixer** was made with two blades and a stand.

• From **1920** soluble **catgut** was used to stitch up wounds.

• 1901 Landsteiner noted the existence of **blood groups**.

• 1903 Einthoven made the **electrocardiograph** which measures the heartbeat.

• 1907 A safe **blood transfusion** was made and **blood tests** began.

Nutrition was better understood after the discovery of **amino acids** and **vitamins**.

• 1921 Banting and Best introduced the life-saving drug **insulin** to treat the disease diabetes.

• 1923 The Marconi company brought out an electronic valve **hearing aid**.

• 1928 Fleming noticed th certain mould slowed the rotting process. This chance covery led to the developm of **penicillin antibiotics** fo the treatment of infection.

Tests with **whooping cough vaccine** proved effective but it was not yet widely used.

• 1902 A newspaper cartoon of 'Teddy' Roosevelt with a grizzly bear cub led to toy bears being called **teddy bears**.

Teddy bear

• 1904 **Double-sided gramophone discs** were made in Germany.

• A **crossword** craze began when the first puzzle appeared in New York newspaper in **1913**.

• The 1920s 'Jazz Age' arrived with blues and jazz music, made popular by records.

• 1914 Walter won a competition for the new sport of **water-skiing**.

• 1917 The **technicolour** film process was invented, and slowly replaced black and white films.

• The worst battle took place in **1916** on the Somme. In 20 weeks 16 km were gained at the cost of a million dead.

• 1905 Johnson invented a **juke box** to play any of 24 records.

• 1908 The first **animated cartoon** was produced by Blackton in the US.

1914 Austria-Hungary's war against Serbia and Germany's invasion of Belgium drew their rivals into battle, with the main war zone being the trenches along the Western Front across Europe. Little territory changed hands, but 10 million died.

• By 1929 the **football pools**, a form of gambling on soccer results, was popular in Britain.

• From 1923 sound-tracks were put on films. The first 'talkie' was Jolson's *The Jazz Singer* in **1927**.

• Dissatisfaction among workers and intellectuals in Russia caused a **revolution** in **1905** and another in 1917 which replaced the Tsars with a Communist state.

Anglo-German rivalry worsened the bitterness in Europe, and there were crises over who had rights to Morocco (**1905 and 1911**) and Bosnia (**1908-9**).

• 1919 The Treaty of Versailles blamed Germany for the war and extracted territory and reparations. In 1920 the League of Nations was set up.

Germany bitterly resented the terms of the Treaty, which sowed the seeds of the Second World War. Under its new socialist government it suffered a currency 'crash' in **1923**.

• In **1929** panic on the Wall Street Stock Market led to banks and businesses failing, causing worldwide **unemploymen**

1900 · 1905 · 1910 · 1915 · 1920 · 1925

Into the modern age

Phonograph and gramophone

Sound consists of vibrations that travel through the air. Early sound-recording equipment relied on this: the phonograph detected these vibrations and turned them into a trace on a solid object such as a sheet of tinfoil or the wax surface of a cylinder.

The phonograph: In 1877 Edison was able to play back sounds 'embossed' through vibrations on to tin foil wrapped round a cylinder

Berliner introduced the use of discs, rather than cylinders. This improved sound quality

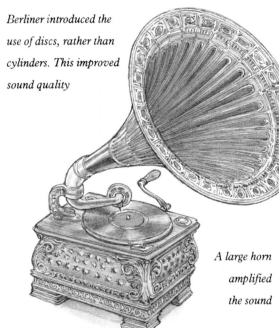

A large horn amplified the sound

The person who came up with this principle was American inventor Thomas Alva Edison in 1877. His phonograph had a diaphragm that vibrated when it picked up a sound. This diaphragm was connected to a stylus (or needle) which cut a groove in the tinfoil on the cylinder. A similar stylus could then be used to play back the sound, which was amplified by a large horn.

Improvements in sound quality and ease of use came with electrical recording, especially when the disc-playing gramophone was introduced by Emile Berliner in 1887.

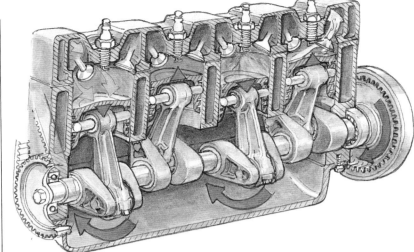

Internal combustion engine

The first *internal* combustion engine (the fuel that burns to make the piston move does so *inside* the cylinder) ran on lighting gas made from coal. It was designed by Frenchman Etienne Lenoir in the 1850s. This was followed by other gas engines that used the four-stroke cycle of operation devised by Alphonse de Rochas in 1862. The future of the internal combustion engine was ensured when German engineer Gottlieb Daimler started to build petrol engines in the 1880s. Karl Benz of Mannheim put petrol engines into vehicles, starting with a motorcycle and tricycle in 1885, and a four-wheeled car in 1886.

Internal combustion works in four stages:
1. Induction (gas and air are let into the cylinder)
2. Compression (the gas and air are compressed and ignited)
3. Power (the expanding gases in the cylinder force the piston down)
4. Exhaust (the burnt fuel is released from the cylinder)

Aeroplane

Many different people were experimenting with heavier-than-air flying machines at the end of the 19th century. But the pioneers who are credited with the first powered, controlled manned flight in a heavier-than-air machine were Wilbur and Orville Wright. The American brothers made their first flight in 1903 at Kitty Hawk, North Carolina. The Wrights' aircraft, *Flyer*, worked because it had a petrol engine with a good power-to-weight ratio, a frame that they had tested carefully, and wings that could be twisted slightly to steer the aircraft and that had the right cross-section to lift it into the air.

Cross section of wing showing how the air gives lift

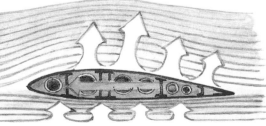

The wing of an aeroplane gives lift because moving air is at lower pressure than still air. The curved cross-section of the wing (called an aerofoil section) pushes up the air passing over the top of the wing, speeding it up. This results in the air above the wing being at lower pressure than the air below. In effect, the wing is sucked upwards from above and pushed up from below.

Did you know that . . .

The Wright brothers gained much of their early practical mechanical know-how from running a bicycle repair shop!

Two Frenchmen, Charles and Émile Pathé, imported a phonograph to attract customers to their tavern. When their customers turned out to be more interested in the phonograph than in eating and drinking, the brothers began to make their own machines, opened a shop to sell them and eventually made their own recordings of popular French singers.

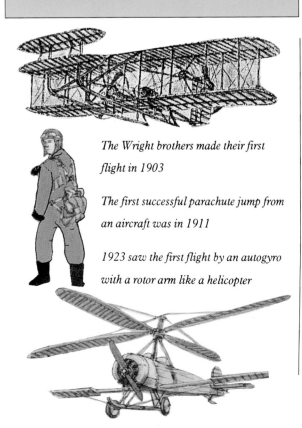

The Wright brothers made their first flight in 1903

The first successful parachute jump from an aircraft was in 1911

1923 saw the first flight by an autogyro with a rotor arm like a helicopter

Mass production

In traditional craft production one worker makes each complete object. In mass production, the manufacturing process is divided up between workers who do different specialized tasks — some will make a particular component, others will do part of the assembly. This greatly speeds up the production process and means that every similar component must be interchangeable.

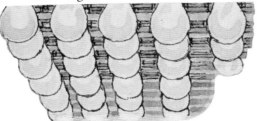

Light bulbs being created en masse. *Ribbons of hot glass were fed along rollers and filled with compressed air*

Mass production began as a response to a sudden demand for a large number of items which, it seemed, could not be met in any other way. One of the first examples was the production of handguns for the American military in the 19th century. Samuel Colt's famous revolvers (first produced in 1835) were made in this way.

Henry Ford's automobile factory

However, the best examples of mass production had to wait until the 20th century, with the coming of the American automobile industry. The greatest pioneer was Henry Ford. He combined mass production, using interchangeable parts, with the idea of a moving assembly line to bring a steady stream of partly finished cars to each worker. The Model T Ford was the first of his vehicles to be produced in this way, in 1908. Since then the method has spread to the production of practically every form of manufactured goods.

Do you know . . . Henry Ford insisted that gearboxes must be delivered in crates of a special size and shape so that he could use them for the car floorboards!

Light bulb

Before a successful light bulb could be made, scientists had to find a way to create a vacuum inside the bulb and find a suitable material for the glowing filament. Two inventors, Joseph Wilson Swan in England and Thomas Alva Edision in the USA, were working on these problems in the 1870s.

Candle and gaslight would become a thing of the past with the invention of the electric light bulb

Both inventors worked along similar lines, Swan using paper as the raw material for his carbon filament, Edison using cotton. Both benefitted from the work of English inventor William Crookes, who devised an efficient way of removing the air from glass containers.

Swan was the first, in 1878, to light his bulb successfully. Edison succeeded in the following year. Initially the two inventors set up rival companies to market their products but eventually they joined forces.

Rocket

A rocket works in a way similar to a jet engine, but carries its own supply of oxygen. This means that it does not need air from the Earth's atmosphere and so is a good vehicle for space travel. Rockets were also used in warfare, at least as early as the 18th century.

The first liquid-propelled rocket was designed by the American R H Goddard in 1926. Goddard saw its potential for space travel, but the German government was quick to adopt it for military use. By 1944 German scientists had designed the V2 ballistic missile, of which some 4,000 were launched during World War II. After the war many people who had worked on the German rockets went to Russia and the USA. The space research programmes of these two countries were helped greatly by these scientists.

Television

One of the biggest problems facing the pioneers of television was how to break down or scan a moving image to make it into a stream of information that could be sent across the airwaves. In the early 20th century two ways of doing this were devised. An electronic method was based on a cathode-ray tube; a mechanical method used a spinning disc pierced with a spiral of holes.

1925 saw the beginnings of television

Scottish inventor John Logie Baird chose the mechanical system and showed his first television pictures in 1925. These pictures were built up in a number of broad vertical strips. Their resolution was very low and the small screen flickered.

The future, however, lay with the electronic scanning system. This produced clearer sharper pictures and, in spite of the fact that Baird made improvements to his mechanical system, the cathode-ray tube was in general use by the mid-1930s.

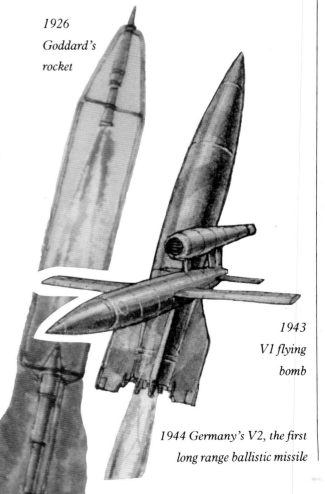

1926 Goddard's rocket

1943 V1 flying bomb

1944 Germany's V2, the first long range ballistic missile

Nuclear fusion

Current nuclear power stations work by harnessing the energy released during nuclear *fission* ('splitting the atom'). In the 1950s the hydrogen bomb showed the potential of combining nuclei in the process called nuclear *fusion*. Since then, scientists have been trying to find ways of harnessing fusion for the peaceful production of energy.

The idea is that two light nuclei (of atoms such as hydrogen or deuterium) combine to form a new stable nucleus. This is lighter than the original two nuclei, so energy is released. The fuel is inexpensive because hydrogen is readily available.

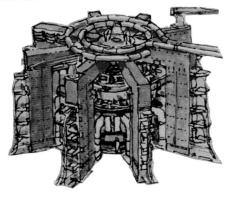

Toros, a magnetic container in which nuclear fusion can take place

However, it has proved very difficult to produce a practical fusion reactor since the first controlled fusion reaction in 1988. For example, the extremely high temperatures involved mean that conventional containers for the reaction are out of the question. Other solutions are being tried, such as containing the nuclei in a magnetic field. Much more work needs to be done before the prospect of cheap, clean nuclear energy becomes a reality.

More about industrial robots

Industrial robots are a far cry from the walking and thinking humanoids of science-fiction.

They are more likely to be 'disembodied' limbs with hydraulically controlled joints.

Highly complex sequences of movements can be programmed into a computer's memory to control the robot's limbs. These limbs have been designed to do a particular job over and over again.

Quartz timepiece

Quartz clocks and watches provide highly accurate timekeeping. Unlike mechanical timepieces they do not need winding and have few moving parts. They rely on the fact that a small crystal of quartz will vibrate minutely at 32,768 times per second when an electric current is applied to it. This current can be supplied by a battery. A microchip detects the vibrations of the crystal and reduces them to a rate of one pulse per second. This one-pulse-per-second signal is used to regulate a small motor that drives the hands around — or to give a digital display.

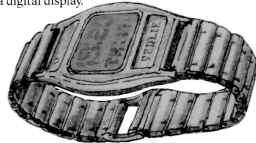

The digital watch first appeared in 1971. Here the pulse is produced in the same way but it is used to activate a changing liquid-crystal display to show the time in figures.

Domestic video recorder

During the 1940s and 1950s experimenters began to find a way of recording television pictures on magnetic tape so that they could be played back like audio recordings. The first machines were designed for use by television companies wanting to broadcast pre-recorded material. The first broadcast was made in 1956 using one of Alexander Poniatoff's Ampex machines.

But these early machines were complex technically and needed vast amounts of tape so they were not suitable for home use. The first domestic video machine was introduced by Philips in 1972. It used tape cassettes that gave a playing time of one hour. A helical scanning mechanism crammed more picture information on to the small tape by laying this information across it in a series of diagonal strips.

Can you find the answers?

Mankind has progressed a long way since the inventions and discoveries on the first page of this book. Using both the book pages and the timeline chart, take a look back into history and see if you can answer these questions.

1 When was the first dug-out canoe used?

2 What natural objects inspired De Maestral to create the first Velcro in 1957?

3 Where does the phrase 'a flash in the pan' come from?

4 Why were revolving doors used in skyscrapers in 1884?

5 How do we think the Ancient Egyptians manoevred the stones into place as the pyramid walls grew higher?

6 Where was Marconi's first morse code signal sent to and from?

7 What was the first submarine called?

8 Who made the first false teeth?

9 Who in 1609 discovered the Moon's craters and a ring around Saturn?

10 When was the first animal launched into outer space?

Compact disc

The compact disc uses digital technology to store and play back sound. The sound is translated into a digital code that is represented by a series of tiny pits in a spiral track on the disc. When the disc is played a laser beam is fired at the spiral track and a light-sensitive cell picks up the reflections. These can then be decoded by a small computer into electrical signals that can be processed and amplified to recreate the original sound. Domestic compact discs and players first appeared on the market in 1980. By 1992 CDs were used in computers.

Where to find the facts

Did you find the answers?

1 There is evidence that the first dug-out canoe was used at least as early as 6300 BC but a paddle dating from 7500 BC suggests they have been around far longer

2 Seed heads of burdock

3 From when the powder in the pan of a flintlock gun sparked but failed to fire the ammunition properly

4 So the doors did not stick shut in the draughts caused by the elevators

5 By creating earth ramps in a spiral around the growing walls

6 From Poldhu in Cornwall, England, across the Atlantic to St Johns, Newfoundland (1901)

7 The Turtle (1775)

8 The Etruscans in about 700 BC

9 Galileo of Italy

10 In November 1957 Laika in Sputnik II was the first 'space dog'. Monkeys were sent into orbit in May 1959.

Glossary

acid chemical substance; it contains hydrogen and is corrosive (eats away other substances)

alloy metal made from a mixture of two or more metals, or a metal and a non-metal

anaesthetic substance which lessens body's sensitivity to pain

atom smallest fragment into which elements can be divided. All substances are made up of atoms, each of which has a central nucleus

axle bar on which a wheel turns or which joins a pair of wheels

bacteria tiny living things which can cause disease

combustion chemical process producing heat and light, normally called burning

composite material made up of two or more substances

compress to squeeze a substance so that it occupies a smaller space

computer a machine, usually electronic, which can store and process words and numbers by using a set of mathematical instructions called a program

conductor substance which lets a form of energy (such as electricity or heat) flow along it

convex a surface which curves outwards (like the surface of a ball)

concave a surface that curves inwards (like the inside surface of a bowl)

crank device which changes one kind of motion into another

data pieces of information

device a tool made to do a particular job

devise to work out a method or plan, to find a way of doing something or solving a problem

electrical current energy in the form of charged electrons which flow through a conductor

electromagnetism the magnetic force produced by an electric current

element substance which cannot be broken down into other simpler substances

energy ability to do work, such as heat, sound, light or motion

engine a machine which converts fuel into power

focus to use a mirror or lens to bend rays of light to concentrate them at a single point

force a push or pull which creates movement or change, such as gravity

friction resistance as the surfaces of two bodies move across or (if liquids or gases are involved) through each other

gear wheel with teeth that fit into and turn other gears; often used to trasnmit energy and drive machines

generator machine which converts energy into electricity

gas substance with widely spaced moving molecules

hydraulic the movement of liquids; water power

lens a transparent substance, curved on one or both sides, that bends light rays to focus them

magnetism force which makes some objects attract others

microchip a tiny piece of an element, such as silicon, containing many electronic circuits and which can store information as electric signals

molecule smallest fragment of a chemical substance, made up of two or more atoms

motor a machine which converts energy already generated into power — usually to produce mechanical motion

patent to obtain the sole right to make and profit from an invention

radiation energy transmitted by rays or waves

spectrum the different colours that make up white light

synthetic not natural; made from chemicals

vacuum space that is completely empty, even of air

valve device which controls flow

vibrate moving backwards and forwards, or up and down, often very quickly

wave the transmission of energy through a substance by disturbing the particles that form it although the substance itself does not move